CW00320549

ORANGUTAN
RESCUE

By Sean Whyte & Alan Knight OBE

G2 Entertainment

Copyright © 2015
First edition published in the UK in 2015
© G2 Entertainment 2015

All rights reserved. No part of this work may be reproduced
or utilized in any form or by any means, electronic or
mechanical, including photocopying, recording or by any
information storage and retrieval system,
without prior written permission of the publisher.

Print Edition ISBN: 978 1 782815 35 8

The views in this book are those of the authors but they are general
views only and readers are urged to consult the relevant and qualified
specialist for individual advice in particular situations.

G2 Entertainment Limited hereby exclude all liability to the extent
permitted by law of any errors or omissions in this book and for any
loss, damage or expense (whether direct or indirect) suffered by a
third party relying on any information contained in this book.

All our best endeavours have been made to secure copyright
clearance but in the event of any copyright owner being
overlooked please go to www.g2ent.co.uk where you
will find all relevant contact information.

G2 Entertainment, 7-8 Whiffens Farm,
Clement street, Hextable, Kent BR8 7PQ

Design By Flokk Creative

Introduction

International Animal Rescue's (IAR) work helping to save orangutans began in late 2009. When IAR heard of the urgent need to help rescue the growing number of orphaned orangutans in West Kalimantan (Indonesian Borneo) there was no time to delay and the charity responded immediately.

Led by the indomitable vet Karmele Llano Sanchez, IAR's orangutan rescue and rehabilitation centre is now the most modern in all of Indonesia with over 80 orangutans in its care. With a team of close to 60 people, mostly Indonesian, supplemented from time to time with overseas volunteers, the centre is making a big difference to the lives of many orangutans that are being rescued and gradually rehabilitated back to protected forest where they are monitored to ensure their future safety.

Saving orangutans, as we shall see, is easier said than done. It's often dangerous, frequently heartbreaking, and always physically demanding. It takes very special, highly skilled people to rescue and rehabilitate orangutans, but these remarkable people acknowledge their work is only possible because of the kind support received from donors and sponsors across the world.

We hope "Orangutan Rescue" will illustrate and explain the work carried out in this remote area of Borneo, introduce the people involved and show how donors' money is being put to excellent use saving these magnificent animals.

Orangutans arrive in rescue centres for one reason. Their forest home has been destroyed, often their mothers have been killed and the babies taken to sell as pets. It's fair to say, every orangutan you see in this book is a victim either of the palm oil industry or the logging industry. Left alone, orangutans would live happily in the forests of Borneo and Sumatra. Sadly, their peace was shattered decades ago. The first threat came from loggers, both legal and illegal, with an eye for a quick profit from the then vast forests spread across Borneo and Sumatra.

The next threat came when land laid bare and abandoned after being logged attracted the attention of the palm oil industry. For at least the last twenty five years forests and wildlife have been decimated. Wildlife not killed for food is instead captured and sold illegally on the black market.

An increasing demand from an ever growing worldwide population for cheap cooking oil, has led to a gold rush fever engulfing Indonesia and Malaysia. Palm oil has become the world's most versatile and profitable vegetable oil. Just as the wood from Borneo found its way into our homes, so has palm oil. It's in biscuits, margarine, soap powder and countless everyday household products. Thankfully, after years of deserved bad publicity, the palm oil industry has begun to mend it ways.

International Animal Rescue is committed to rescuing and rehabilitating as many orangutans as possible and giving them a second chance to live safely in a secure natural habitat. Over 100 orangutans have been rescued in the first five years.

For more information on orangutans and how you can adopt one for yourself or as a special gift to a friend or loved one, please visit **www.internationalanimalrescue.org**

Acknowledgements: The authors would like to acknowledge the help received in putting this book together. Photographers have permitted the free use of their photographs. IAR staff and volunteers including Karmele Llano Sanchez, Lisa Burtenshaw, Gail Campbell-Smith, Christine Nelson, Paloma Corbi and Lis Key all helped with research. Margaret Whyte assisted with editing. We also thank the publisher Jules Gammond for his enthusiastic support. International Animal Rescue would like to thank The Forestry Department of West Kalimantan, Balai Konservasi Sumber Daya Alam (BKSDA), Richard and Robin Zimmerman at Orangutan Outreach for their financial and moral support, The Orangutan Project who funded IAR from day one and continue to support the charity's work and The Arcus Foundation for their continued support. Most of all, a big thank you to the Michael Uren Foundation for their financial support in building the rescue centre and purchasing the land and the many people who have supported International Animal Rescue with donations and/or time, because without you none of the orangutans you see in this book could have been helped.

Photographs: The authors and publisher would like to thank the following photographers for donating the use of their photographs.

Alejo Sabugo: pages 8, 9, 10, 11, 21 (RHS), 29, 65, 76, 98 Argitoe Ranting/IAR: pages 12 (left) 67, 68, 69, 70, 71, 86, 87, 113, 114 Julie O'Neill: pages 15, 22, 23, 25, 28, 36, 37, 47, 75, 77, 108, 108, Roger Allen: pages 18, 19, 41, 42, 43, 74, 106, 136 ShadowView: pages 39, 40 Noah De Clair: pages 80, 81 Thomas Burns: pages; front cover, 14, 16, 17, 20, 27, 31, 32, 44, 48, 52, 53, 54, 55, 57 (rescue photos), 58, 59, 84, 85, 124, 130 Paloma Corbi: pages 50, 115, 116 Lisa Burtenshaw: pages; title page, 24, 101, 117, 118, 119, 120, 121, 122, 123, 131, 132, 138 (lower photo), 140, 141, 142 Gavin Parsons: pages 34, 35 Feri Latief: page 49 Karmele Llano Sanchez/IAR: pages 99, 100 All other photographs are courtesy of International Animal Rescue.

Contents

The Orangutan

In Malay language orangutan means "man of the forest." Sharing 96.4% of our genes, orangutans are remarkably intelligent.

There are two species of orangutan, Sumatran and Bornean.

The largest tree-dwelling animal on earth, adult males can weigh up to 120 kilos. Females are a lot smaller and weigh about 45 kilos. They make nests in the tree tops of the rainforest by bending over branches to make the frame for a bed on which they then lay smaller, leafy branches to form a 'mattress'. The bed is also used to rest in during the daytime. Females normally give birth to one baby approximately every seven to eight years, which then stays with its mother for about seven years.

They are known to eat over 300 different food types, consisting mostly of fruit, with figs and durian being firm favourites,

supplemented with tree bark, leaves, insects and even birds' eggs. Possessing an excellent memory, orangutans are able to make a 'mental-map' of the forests which enhances their ability to find fruit in season.

Although they spend most of their time in trees, Bornean orangutans, especially, are known sometimes to come to the ground in search of food.

Despite being a legally protected species throughout its range, over the last few decades at least 2000 orangutans a year have been killed or captured and sold into the illegal pet and zoo trade.

Scientists estimate 10,000 orangutans remain in Sabah (Malaysian Borneo), 3000 in Sarawak (Malaysian Borneo), 6600 in Sumatra and 50,000 in Kalimantan (Indonesia Borneo). One hundred years ago there may have been 250,000 orangutans.

Most of the remaining orangutans live in unprotected forest, leaving the species in grave danger due to relentless conversion of forests to oil palm plantations. The killing of orangutans for food across a large swathe of Kalimantan is a relatively recent and worrying discovery currently thought to account for as many as 1000 deaths a year. Considered a solitary animal with a lifespan of 45-50 years, orangutans pose no threat to humans.

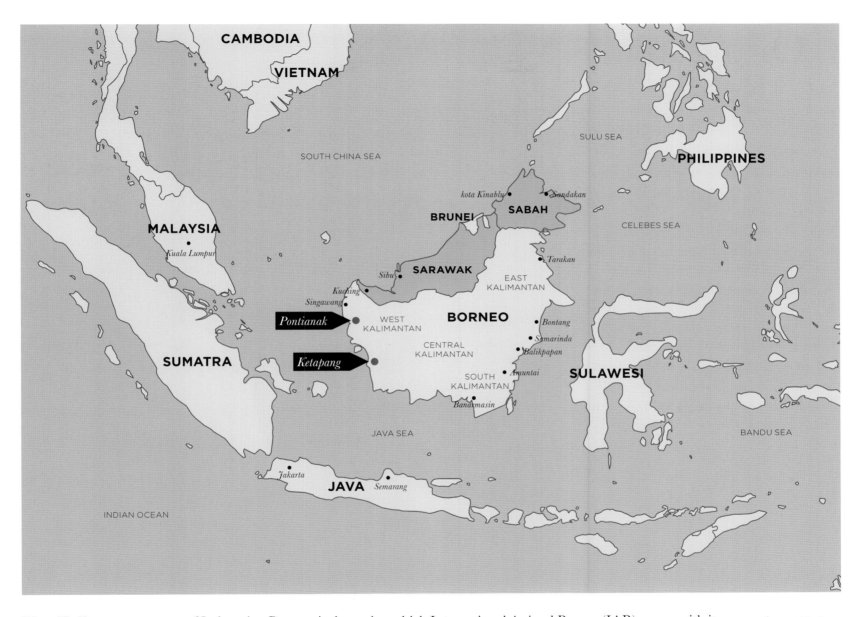

West Kalimantan, a part of Indonesian Borneo, is the region which International Animal Rescue (IAR) covers with its orangutan rescue work. Stretching to just over 147,000 sq km, West Kalimantan has a tropical climate with mountains, forests and swamps. It's a mineral rich area with mining for bauxite and coal industries now very big employers. Mining, coupled with logging and the rapid expansion of oil palm plantations, has had a devastating effect on all wildlife; none more so than orangutans.

Orangutan Rescue

The emergency call came in: four starving orangutans in urgent need of rescuing after their forest home had been bulldozed by a palm oil company.

Having been sedated, this orangutan with a baby clinging to her back, had to be carried by Argitoe, head of the rescue team, across very rough terrain in monsoon rain before being placed into a translocation cage and moved to a safe forest. Vet Syifa Sidik is protecting the mother's eyes and nose from the rain. It can never be stressed enough how physically and emotionally hard the work of saving orangutans on the front-line often is.

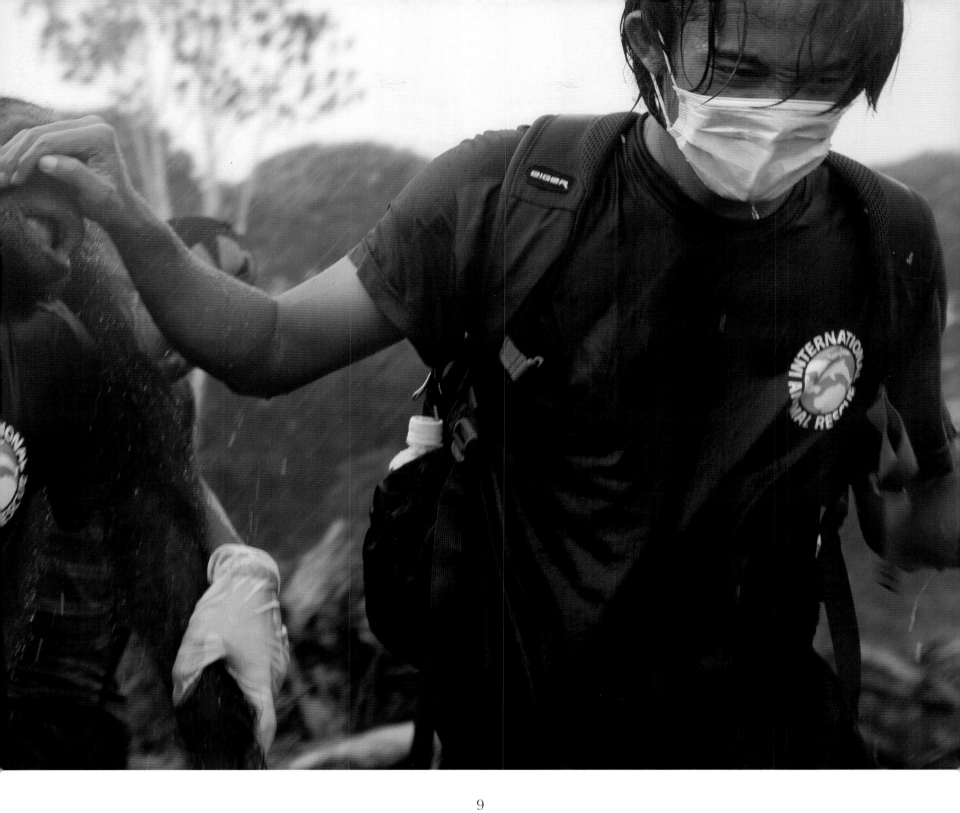

All four orangutans had gone through long periods of starvation before IAR was called to rescue them. This female had already lost her baby before the rescue team arrived.

It requires a skilled marksman to hit an orangutan with an anaesthetic dart at this distance without damaging any of its vital organs.

This frightened and hungry mother with her baby in one of the last few trees remaining also had to be darted and caught.

Once the anaesthetic begins to take effect the adult orangutan may climb down 20 - 30 metres to the waiting rescue team. Often a drowsy orangutan will fall through the branches and have to be caught in a net.

Once safely on the ground this mother and baby were found to have sustained no injuries. They were quickly moved to another forest to live out their lives, free of interference from loggers and palm oil companies.

How it all began

IAR vet and programme director Karmele Llano Sanchez is monitoring *JoJo's* heart rate while he is sedated on the day of his rescue in the nearby town of Pontianak. He had spent more than 10 years chained to a pole over an open sewer in a private home. *JoJo* was the first orangutan IAR rescued in West Kalimantan and he was also the most powerful reason for establishing the IAR orangutan rescue centre in this province.

Since his arrival at the centre in 2009 *JoJo's* appearance has changed beyond recognition! He has grown into a handsome mature male with huge cheekpads. He is an inquisitive character and loves to sit at the front of his large cage and observe all the goings-on at the centre.

When *Bunga* arrived at IAR's orangutan rescue centre in November 2009 she was estimated to be about two and a half years old and had been kept in a cage in a family's garden.

They claimed to have found her wandering around near their home about three months earlier and decided to keep her.

At first *Bunga* was very frightened and timid. She constantly tried to cling on to the keepers and hide behind them. Everything scared her, even the sound of the birds squawking in the trees! Even now when she goes outside to play she will cling on to the carer for the first few minutes and does not want to let go. She is extremely affectionate and gradually growing in confidence. *Bunga* loves climbing, swinging and playing with the leaves. Look at the size of those hands!

Bunga (please see previous page and front cover)

Ongky, seen here with his 'babysitter', made history by becoming the first orangutan confiscation resulting in the owner being caught, prosecuted and ultimately jailed. Local government forestry department staff arrested the owner carrying *Ongky* in a sack in the nearby town of Pontianak.

The role of the babysitter is one of surrogate mother, taking care of the baby orangutans until they are able and ready to move to 'forest school' where they spend more time climbing trees and learning to become self sufficient. The mask is worn to prevent any cross infection.

Rickina was confiscated from a private home.
The scar on her forehead is from a wound sustained when her mother was killed with a machete.
Rickina would have been clinging to her at the time. Both are victims of the palm oil industry.

Rickina (with the scar) and her best friend *Rocky*. Both are about two to three years old. At this tender age baby orangutans seek out companionship at every opportunity. Had their mothers not been killed both these babies would still be attached or very close to them every minute of the day for the first seven years of their lives.

Exhausted after a bout of playful activity at the rehabilitation centre there is only one thing left these two close friends can do. Sleep! Even when asleep, they like to be in close contact.

17

Mely had been kept as a family pet and fed scraps of food. Despite being tethered to a short chain around her neck for some 15 years and being regularly teased by both children and adults, not with malice but out of ignorance, she has remained a very gentle orangutan. In October 2010 with help from readers of the Daily Mail, IAR with the assistance of the local forestry police launched a rescue mission and brought *Mely* back to the rehabilitation centre. *(See opposite page)*.

Free of her chain and from being tormented, *Mely* can now relax and dream of a much happier future.

Pelangi (Indonesian for 'rainbow') was a two year old orangutan when she was confiscated She had been bought as a pet for $50, kept in a bird cage, fed dried fruit and dried milk and dressed like a human baby.

All rescues require government paperwork to be completed, in this instance, at the local forestry police office.

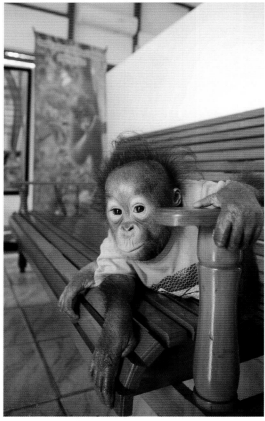

Not lacking in confidence, once out of quarantine at the rehabilitation centre *Pelangi* was able to move on to climbing the lower branches of trees.

Malnourished and bewildered *Tribune* had been kept as a pet in a cardboard box until rescued by IAR.

The baby orangutan was found by a villager on the estate of a palm oil plantation company.

Since being rescued and cared for by IAR, *Tribune* is now barely recognisable.

Noel was captured and locked up by locals after his forest home was destroyed and his mother killed during the construction of a new palm oil plantation. A local tried to sell him to IAR, but instead a team from the charity made their way into the plantation and confiscated baby Noel.

Noel tucking into some tasty leaves. In the wild orangutans eat several hundred different food items. In the IAR centre they are offered as wide a range of leaves, fruits and vegetables as possible and this extends to about 25 different fruits and 15 different types of vegetables.

While indoors the babies need to wear nappies much as human babies do - to keep them and the area they play in clean and free from infection.

If food was only provided at ground level the baby orangutans would be unlikely to climb trees and search for it by themselves when they are returned to the forest.

Staff at the rehabilitation centre ensure each baby orangutan receives enough food, while also encouraging them to climb and search for food treats hidden in the trees of the secure area at the centre.

Prior to confiscation *Butan* had been kept as a pet. When rescued he was found to be suffering from cerebral malaria, malnutrition and hair loss - more dead than alive. *Butan* responded well to intensive care and has gone on to become one of the most successful nest builders in forest school. When adult he will be capable of opening a coconut like this one with his bare hands.

Oscarina was aged about two to three years old when her owner handed her over to IAR because she had skin problems due to an allergy caused by being fed fried prawn pies. Eradicating this skin condition required her to be bathed regularly.

Oscarina (r) with her close companion *Pedro* (l)

All orangutans are by nature curious. They will investigate anything new to see what opportunities it might present for play or food. These two youngsters (l-r *Rickina and Rocky*) soon discovered lots of fun could be had playing in sand set aside for construction work at the transit centre.

With the former transit centre facility in the background (the new purpose built centre opened in 2013) this babysitter has more than her hands full with orangutans seeking attention. Clinging to their adopted mother comes very naturally to orangutans as this is what they do until about seven years of age with their real mothers in the forest.

When *Butan* has moisturiser applied to
his skin others take a great interest.
At any one time there might be 15
orangutans in 'baby school.'

Babysitters are all local people trained
by International Animal Rescue.

This was to become one of the more dangerous rescue attempts. On arrival at this property the IAR team and forestry police were confronted by an alcoholic owner who threatened to kill both the orangutan and the rescue team with a machete.

Chained by a leg *Ucil* was only able to move one metre from his crate.

To secure his release from the aggressive owner the rescue team needed to make a second visit. This time they brought with them a much larger team of 12 forestry police rangers from the nearby town of Pontianak.

The confiscation went ahead and *Ucil* is now at the IAR rehabilitation centre. *(continued opposite)*

When *Ucil* arrived at the clinic he was found to be bloated and constipated. His owner had been giving him alcohol as well as unsuitable food.

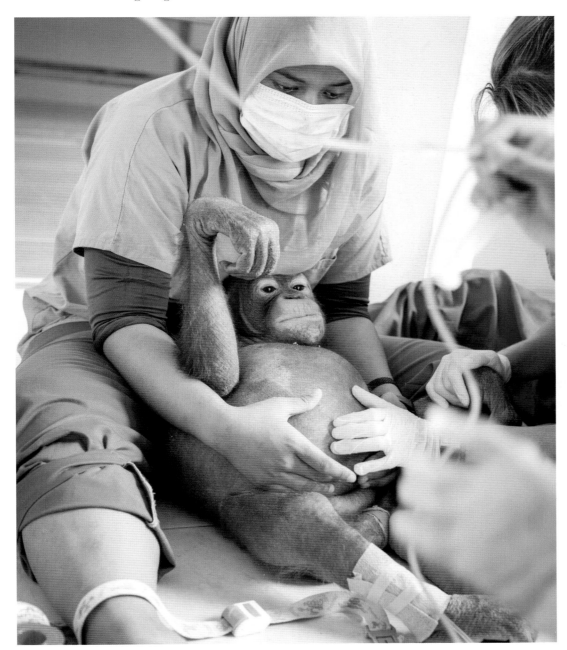

After spending time in the clinic *Ucil* went on to make a full recovery.
(please see overleaf)

Orangutans learn from experience as well as watching others. Exploring a pool of water for the first time can be great fun as well as an opportunity to cool off in the heat of the day, as *Ucil* discovered.

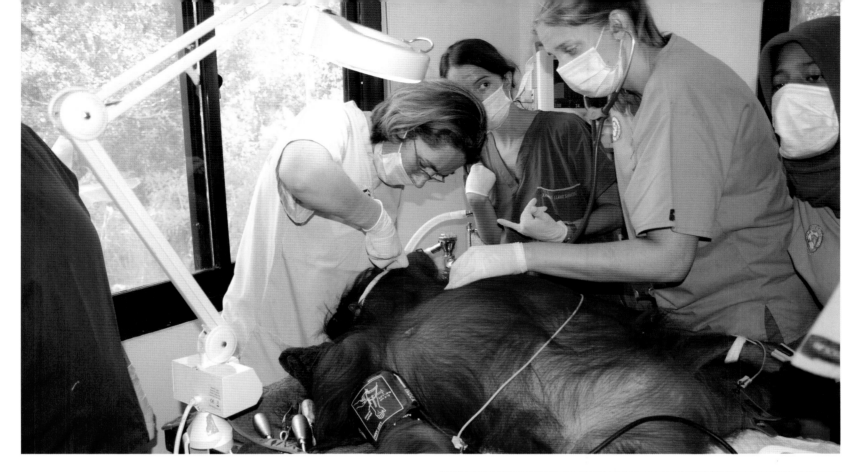

Pingky was one of the earlier and older orangutans received by IAR.

When she arrived at the centre and received her initial health check it became apparent *Pingky* was suffering severe dental decay, most likely caused by being fed sweets and given fizzy drinks.

This required a complex dental procedure involving seven extractions and three root canal treatments. From left to right vets Lisa Milella, Karmele Llano Sanchez, Christine Nelson and Ayu Budi Handayani. Lisa is a dental specialist from the UK and has donated her time to IAR for many years and is now a Trustee of the UK charity.

After her operation *Pingky* is looking a lot happier and healthier. This is not a contrived photo!

Sadly, until IAR set up a base in Ketapang this was not an uncommon sight outside private homes throughout West Kalimantan. Fortunately for *Jingo* he had spent his last day in this cage (*Please see opposite page*).

Once confiscated by the local forestry police *Jingo* was soon on his way to IAR's transit centre where he was formally handed over (see below) to to the safekeeping of project director and vet Karmele Llano Sanchez.

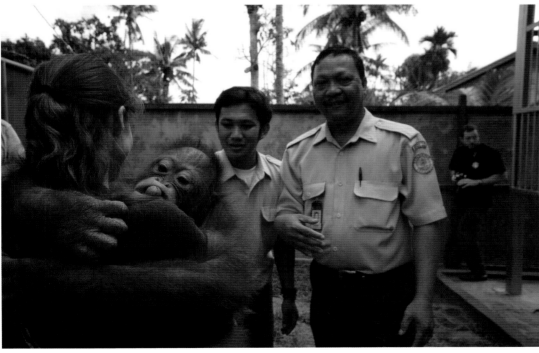

IAR was first alerted to *Karmila* by local group Yayasan Palung who accompanied the IAR team and the local forestry police during the confiscation. *Karmila* was being kept by a very poor family who claimed they had found her in a palm oil plantation. Once clear of quarantine she settled in well at the transit centre.

Dinner time before this group settle down for the night at the transit centre. They are all now in forest school and spend their days from 6am to 6pm clambering around the trees gaining knowledge and learning new skills they will need when they are returned to the wild.

By 2013 IAR had outgrown the transit centre taken over four years previously from a local environmental group.

Thanks to the generosity of supporters and benefactors it was possible to buy land surrounded by forest outside Ketapang town and construct a purpose built orangutan rescue and rehabilitation centre. First to be moved were 18 curious baby orangutans.

The only practical way to move the orangutans was by road. Protected from both sun and rain they settled down for the short ride.

Aerial views of the new centre taken from a drone. An orchard on the left is used to grow fruit for the orangutans, The buildings in the distance are staff accommodation on the left and administration office to the right.

View from the rehabilitation centre's front gate looking forward.

A one hectare enclosure used as baby school for the youngest orangutans.

This is the first six hectare island created at the orangutan rehabilitation centre for use by the orangutans. The canals were dug by IAR to prevent the orangutans from escaping.

The ongoing challenge is to keep water in the canal all year round and deep enough to discourage any orangutan from attempting to cross it.

Exercise and socialisation areas at the new IAR rescue centre consist of 'baby school' and 'forest school'. Forest school (above),
is where the older and more confident orangutans are taken every day to build up their strength through climbing trees.
At the end of a long day they can choose either to return to the centre for the night or remain in the forest and build their own night nest.

As the evening draws in most of the forest school orangutans choose to accept a lift back to the centre from veterinarians Christine Nelson, Adi Irawan and helpers. By now tired and hungry, the orangutans behave well in the knowledge their evening meal and good night's sleep awaits them.

Although undeniably cute looking these faces mask a lot of suffering and distress. Each of these baby orangutans would have been clinging tightly to its mother's chest when she was killed.

In most cases the mother would have been shot high up in a tree, falling perhaps 60 feet through branches to the ground with her baby which was then taken from the dead body and sold as a pet.

It's often months later before IAR is alerted to the baby's presence in a private home and a rescue mission can be mounted with the local forestry police.

It's always a good sign to see youngsters like *Gembar* examining and probing wood, much as their wild relatives would do, in the hope of finding insects to eat.

'*Bob*' as he became known, had been kept as a pet in this makeshift cage.

The owner was very angry and unwilling to give up the young orangutan and it took the police and forestry department (BKSDA) many hours to persuade him to surrender his pet.

Safely in the hands of vet Ayn Budi Handayani, *Bob* was taken to the rescue centre where he is now enjoying the company of other baby orangutans in baby school.

When confiscated more often than not the orangutans are in need of a bath. Their bodies are sometimes covered in dirt and even faeces from having been kept in unclean cages. A bath also removes any unwanted insect life which may have attached itself to the baby. Most baby orangutans enjoy the water and attention. *(please see opposite page for a cleaner and slightly older Cemong.)*

Cemong looking cleaner, a little older and ready to pose for photos.

Prior to confiscation *Lasmi* had been kept illegally as a pet by the local chief of police.

With their forest home replaced by oil palm plantations, this mother and baby were found by villagers searching for food.
In a panic the villagers trapped the mother with baby clinging to her chest, and proceeded to tie her up in ropes. Worse was to come.

Before the rescue team arrived the villagers had dragged the mother away and drowned her. The baby was rescued and named *Peni*.
Understandably, she was very traumatised, angry even, and remained so throughout her rehabilitation. *(continued overleaf)*

Having made a remarkable recovery from her ordeal (see previous page) *Peni* has since been released into a secure forest where she is monitored daily by IAR staff. Here she can be seen below *Helen*, another rescued orangutan with a traumatic past but now doing well.

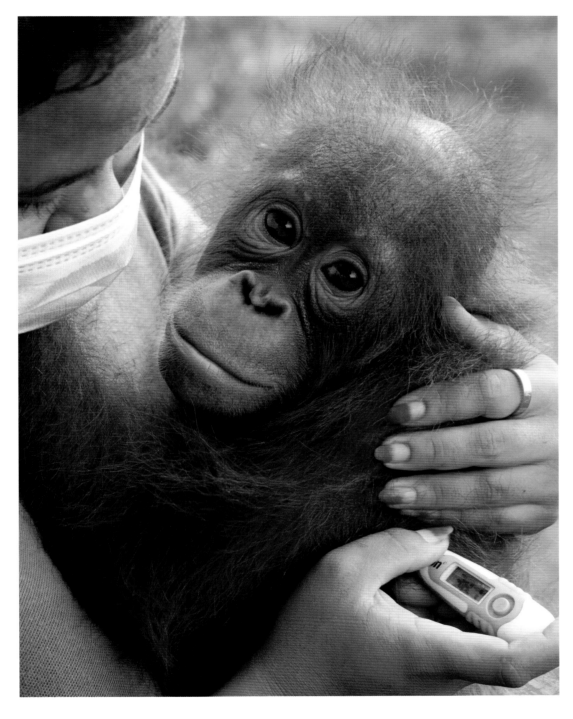

Lady is having her temperature measured. She was rescued from the camp of a Chinese bauxite mine. A wise and very inquisitive orangutan, she is now one of the first to come and check out anything new at the centre. *Lady* gets on well with all the other orangutans, is a good climber and spends much of her time high in the trees.

Onyo is a sweet natured orangutan. He was aged around 12-18 months old when rescued. He had been kept as a pet by a man who fed him on mostly milk and rice. *Onyo* loves to climb and makes friends easily with other baby orangutans, particularly *Rickina*. Both like to play and climb, and light up when they see a camera!

Exhausted from playing *Rickina* (l) with the scar on her forehead and *Onyo* (r) will be being watched over by their babysitter to ensure no harm comes to them while they sleep.

The rescue team were called out to a report of a sub-adult orangutan named *Ael* chained and being tormented beside a road. Villagers claimed they captured her wandering around near a farm, presumably looking for food because her forest home had been cut down.

The good condition of *Ael's* hair and body suggested she had not been held like this for long. *(continued overleaf)*

Most villagers rarely see a wild orangutan and they are not cruel by nature. They sometimes succumb on the spur of the moment to the temptation of either buying a baby orangutan or, as in this instance, tormenting one to show off to their friends. Educating village people and children in particular is, as we shall see later, a very important component of IAR's work.

Before *Ael* could be helped she first had to be anaesthetised. Only then could she be examined closely by IAR vet Karmele Llano Sanchez and freed from the rope around her waist. Seemingly none the worse for her ordeal, it was decided the best thing was to release *Ael* into a safe forest as soon as possible after further health checks back at the rehabilitation centre's clinic.

Ael released with another orangutan, *Sukma*, for company.

Marie (top) with *Onyo* at the beginning of a long journey getting to know their own strengths as well as those of supporting branches, what tastes nice and what doesn't. Experience and skills they would otherwise have learnt from their mothers.

Onyo in full 'flight' between trees shows he is learning fast and growing in confidence. This is behaviour the rehabilitation centre team like to see because preparing rescued orangutans, wherever possible, for a life back in the forest is the ultimate goal.

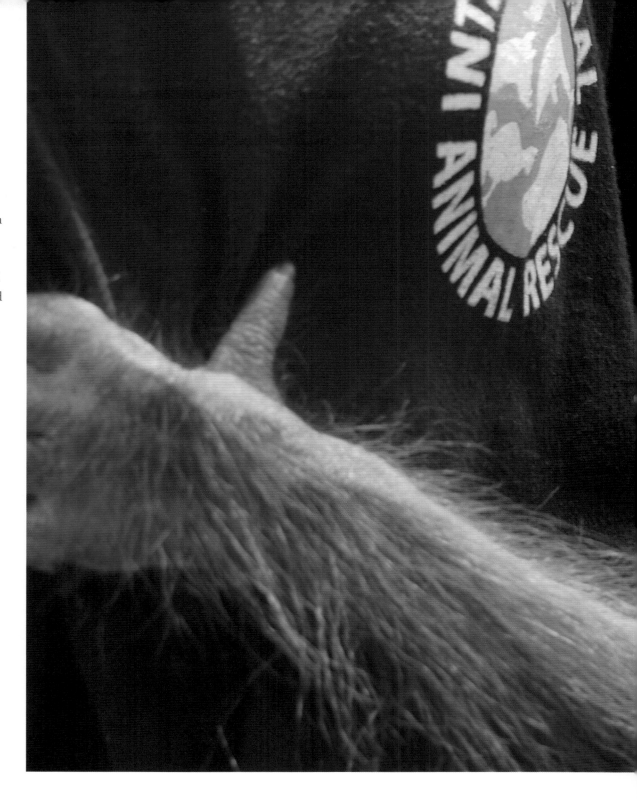

Forestry officials alerted the rescue team to *Monti* being kept as a family pet in a remote rural location.

It took several days to track her down. When questioned, her owner claimed his family had only taken in this tiny orangutan after finding her all alone in the jungle. A mother will never leave her baby alone like that, so the only plausible explanation could be someone, possibly the owner himself, had killed *Monti's* mother. *(continued overleaf)*

Monti soon settled in and began to enjoy her new life at the rehabilitation centre. *(please see opposite)*

Monti (see opposite page) and what a difference four years make! This also illustrates the reality faced years later by people who buy cute-looking baby orangutans. When they become this large they can no longer be handled, outgrow their cage, require a lot of feeding and often become sick.

Monti now loves nothing more than to find a comfy branch to sit on while devouring a juicy fruit.

Readers, you might like to think of your own caption for this photograph!

Rescuing an orangutan from a private home in a remote village often requires the IAR rescue team to take to the water. Apart from the likelihood of being soaked through by a sudden rainstorm, you can never be sure of the reception you will receive from someone whose cherished family pet you are about to confiscate. The owner can sometimes be hostile even though police always attend confiscations.

When the rescue team reached its destination (see opposite) they were alarmed at the condition of the orangutan they found chained to the side of a house. *Bujing* had lost most of his hair due to malnutrition. Although the team estimated him to be five years old he was very small for his age because malnutrition had impaired his growth.

Had *Bujing* been a normal strong and healthy orangutan it would have been unwise if not impossible to take him away in an open boat. A sturdy cage is often necessary for the safety of the team and orangutan. On this occasion *Bujing* was too weak to cause any problems on the way to the rehabilitation centre.

Normally the rescue team is called out to oil palm plantations. However, on this occasion the team responded to a call to remove an adult male orangutan from the few remaining trees around an enormous but failed rice growing area. The ground beneath them was waterlogged and a river and canal had to be crossed. This was to prove to be a very physically challenging rescue operation. *(continued opposite)*

Once the rescue team found him they needed to devise a plan to get this scared and large orangutan to the ground without injury to either the animal or its rescuers.

Firing an anaesthetic dart into a moving animal 20 metres up in a tree takes a keen eye and a lot of experience, but it's the only way. Rescue missions like this one are almost always in remote locations away from back up, carried out under an oppressive heat whilst you are standing in either mud or water – sometimes both. If it rains, as it often does, you get soaked from head to foot.

Can you spot the orangutan in the tree?
(continued overleaf)

Partially sedated, when this orangutan descended the tree he fell into a canal. Project director and vet Karmele Llano Sanchez jumped in and managed to save him from drowning. Once out of the water this large male needed to be checked over by Karmele assisted by vet Christine Nelson and their assistants. Part of the process involves inserting a microchip to help identify this orangutan in the event he is captured again elsewhere.

With both vets satisfied he was free from injuries, on this occasion it was decided the best thing was to take this large male orangutan by boat to a safe forest about one hour away. *(continued overleaf)*

Carrying an 80kg orangutan in a 45kg metal crate through steaming forest to the waiting boat requires strength and dedication. Lifting the crate above head height while standing in muddy water shows the commitment and determination of the rescue team to save each and every orangutan.

(please see opposite for the release)

After a one hour boat ride the orangutan is awake, able to leave his crate and climb directly into the trees which now form part of his new home. Another successful rescue mission.

Baby *Pedro* had been kept in a village far north of the IAR centre in Ketapang. Villagers handed him over to local WWF staff. They in turn handed *Pedro* to the local forestry police, who then put him on a plane to Ketapang where he was received by the local forestry police (protocol has to be followed) and subsequently handed over to IAR. Considering his journey *Pedro* arrived calm and in good health. *(please see opposite page)*

Pedro has since grown into a strong and healthy orangutan who is not exactly camera shy.

Lady (left) was about a year old when she was brought to the centre by the forestry police. She is wise, very inquisitive, always the first to check out anything new and she gets on well with the other orangutans. *Lady* has become a good climber and now spends much of her time high in the trees. *Cemong* was about two years old and weighed 8kg. when he arrived at the rehabilitation centre. He came from an area that had been cleared for a palm oil plantation. His mother had already been killed by the time he was found.

First reported to IAR by a forest ranger, *Gunung* was about five months old when rescued from the nearby Gunung Palung National Park.

An emergency pack of essential medical equipment donated by OVAID (see opposite) is kept ready for the rescue team to take with them at a moment's notice. Vet Ayu is happily checking all the items.

Nigel Hicks founder of Orangutan Veterinary Aid (OVAID) donates more veterinary supplies to the vets at the rehabilitation centre.

(l-r) Vets; Manuel Millanes, Richa Irawan, Christine Nelson, Ayu Budi Handayani, Adi Irawan, Nigel Hicks.

If you would like to donate veterinary supplies to International Animal Rescue please contact **www.ovaid.org**

When IAR received a report of a large orangutan kept as a pet 150 kilometres north of their base in Ketapang it required a flight and then gruelling hours by road before the rescue team and forestry police arrived at the house of a former soldier. As *Kiki* the orangutan had become older and stronger he was too much to handle and the owner decided to surrender him.

According to the owner he had kept *Kiki* for 13 years in a cage which rescuers noticed had a thick 'carpet' of rubbish and faeces covering the floor that *Kiki* also had to sleep on. *(please see opposite)*

Kiki was small for his age, probably due to malnutrition and lack of exercise. IAR vet Karmele Llano Sanchez and her assistant move him into a travelling cage for the long journey to the rescue centre.

Fortunately *Kiki* had a very calm temperament. During the 12 hour boat ride back to the rehabilitation centre he was a model passenger, never displaying any bad temper and he did what the vet asked of him.

The local forestry police attend all such rescues. Owners are normally given a firm warning about the illegality of keeping orangutans as pets.

The story from the owner of *Dio* is that he bought him from a hunter who had killed his mother for food. *Dio* would also have been killed but for the offer of $50 to buy him as a pet. With a bullet still in his left eye, probably from the same gun that killed his mother, he had received no veterinary treatment and was permanently chained by his neck to a pole.

Despite knowing it is illegal to buy and keep an orangutan, during the confiscation the owner told the rescue team and forestry police he would not hesitate to buy another.

The local forestry police chief taking legal possession of *Dio* before handing him over to IAR.

Anjas was three and a half years old when surrendered to the local forestry department. He had spent most of his life being treated like a human baby, wearing clothes and having daily baths. His diet was rice, vegetables, sweet tea and milk, which caused him to have a rectal prolapse. Fortunately he has since recovered. *Anjas* has an old injury to his foot, leaving him unable to use one of his toes. Otherwise he has adjusted to life as an orangutan very well and now enjoys climbing trees and getting dirty.

Galang is yet another victim of the palm oil industry. When rescued he was already used to humans. Always curious, he is taking an interest in what volunteer vet Micah Jensen from New Zealand is preparing for him. *(please see opposite page for an update on Galang)*

Returned to good health, *Galang* is now able to enjoy time in the forest though still under supervision

Loading an empty transportation cage onto a forestry police vehicle before departing on a fourteen hour drive.

On arrival an all too familiar scene confronted the rescue team. *Wawa* had been fed rice, vegetables, rendang (an Indonesian spicy meat dish) and coffee. He was small for his age of between five and six years, with very little hair and poor skin. *Wawa* is being given electrolyte, a rehydration fluid, to drink.

An almost bald *Wawa* could only wonder who these kind strangers were.

IAR were not leaving without him. His life was about to be turned around for the better.

Confiscated, *Wawa* was now on the way to a new and vastly better life at the IAR rehabilitation centre.

Pak Agus Setiyoko was the Police Chief of Ketapang. He lent his support to a local awareness campaign highlighting the importance of orangutans and how habitat loss can lead to conflict situations. The poster describes orangutans as the 'keepers of the forest ecosystem' and they deserve our protection. It also gives the International Animal Rescue Rapid Response Rescue Team Hotline Number.

AKBP. Agus Setiyoko. S. Ik. Kapolres Ketapang sedang menyapa orangutan di Pusat Rehabilitasi Orangutan YIARI, Sei Awan, Ketapang.

ORANGUTAN
adalah warga kita juga,
MARI LINDUNGI!

Orangutan adalah binatang yang dilindungi Undang-Undang. Ketika tempat hidupnya terganggu, penjaga ekosistem hutan ini dapat berkonflik dengan manusia. Apabila terjadi hal tersebut, segera kontak: 0811 5777173

POLRES KETAPANG
KALIMANTAN BARAT

INTERNATIONAL ANIMAL RESCUE
Yayasan IAR
Indonesia
internationalanimalrescue.org

The long, clean hair on this tiny baby suggests he had been recently captured. His owner claimed to have killed and eaten *Puyol's* mother. The rescue team found him with a rope around his neck, desperately in need of a drink as well as being skinny and quite wild by nature. *Puyol* was confiscated and taken to the IAR rehabilitation centre.

To encourage the rescued orangutans to forage for themselves, honey is one of a variety of foods concealed in their exercise area. By using a stick as a tool, honey can be extracted from a hole in this branch.

Having probed the hole and discovered honey, the orangutan has learnt a very important lesson while enjoying a tasty treat!

When rescued *Melki* was aged about three years old. On arrival at the rescue centre he was devoid of most natural orangutan survival skills, including the ability to climb. Over time *Melki's* confidence has grown and he is now a skilled climber.

He is now by far the biggest and naughtiest juvenile in the forest group and can be found by following the cracking sound of the small trees he uses for travelling. Although he is quite a muscular boy, he is very gentle with the youngest ones and even looks after them during rainstorms.

This very sick orangutan had been caught in a snare. He was trapped and in excruciating pain by a wire around one wrist. The snare had been set by a farmer hoping to catch deer or wild pigs. Fearful of being punished for trapping an orangutan, the farmer did not at first alert anyone to its desperate situation.

After about ten days, in which time *Pelangsi's* hand had lost all blood circulation, a friend of the farmer went to the Forestry Department, and they called in International Animal Rescue. Working outside in a makeshift theatre three vets immediately got to work saving *Pelangsi*. *(see opposite)*

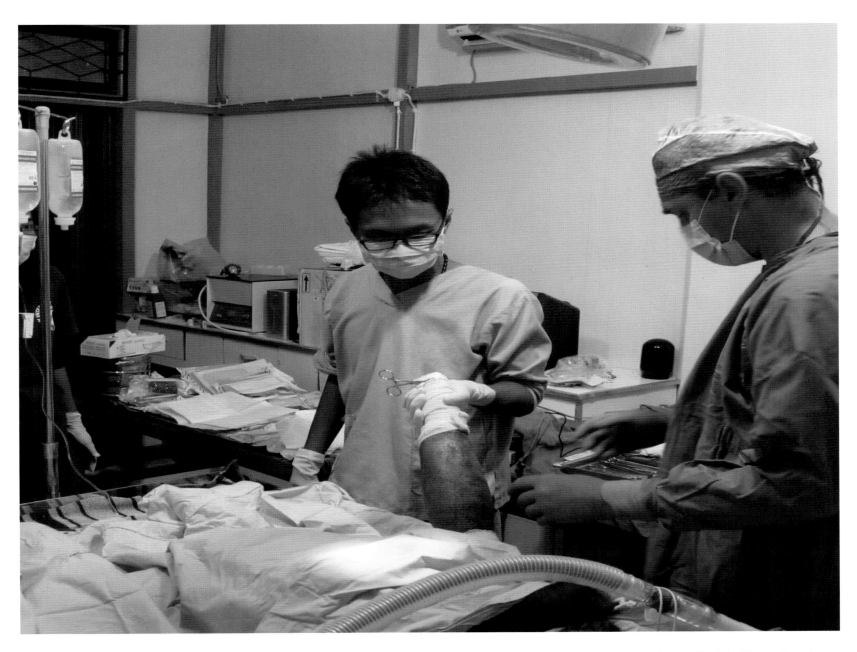

One month later the IAR medical team, led by wildlife specialist vet Dr Paolo Martelli (Chief Veterinarian of Ocean Park in Hong Kong), carried out a complex and lengthy surgical procedure to amputate *Pelangsi's* hand which had suffered extensive damage and could not be saved. *(continued overleaf)*

Pelangsi recovering after the medical procedure to amputate his right hand and forearm

The use of leaves is entirely his choice. In the wild orangutans build a night-nest from branches and the leaves are used both for bedding and protection against rain. *(please see opposite page)*

Six months post-operation *Pelangsi* was considered to be healthy and strong enough to be released. Even without one hand he could climb and feed himself. A suitable forest was found and returning *Pelangsi* to the wild got underway.

Reaching the forest began with a ride on the back of a local forestry police vehicle. Then a speedboat trip up river before transferring to a local villager's boat better able to access this remote release area. Under a burning sun and high humidity this was a physically demanding task. *(continued overleaf)*

After a long trek through the jungle *Pelangsi's* release into the forest was imminent. *(please see opposite)*

As the long, hot day drew to a close *Pelangsi* was released and free once again to roam the forests. The exhausted but elated IAR repatriation team look on before making their own long journey home.

The owner of *Ceria* claimed to have found her injured on the ground in an oil palm plantation a week earlier, but changed his story a few times during the rescue operation.

In the early part of 2015 news of little *Budi's* suffering and ultimate rescue made world headlines. For the first year of his life *Budi* had been kept as a pet in a chicken cage and fed entirely on condensed milk. The owner had informed her local forestry police that she was willing to hand over a small baby orangutan she had been keeping as a pet. She also admitted that the baby was very sick. The IAR rescue team responded immediately. After a journey of more than 10 hours by boat and road, *Budi* arrived safely at the rehabilitation centre. At first *Budi* didn't even have the strength to sit up on his own without support. *(please see overleaf)*

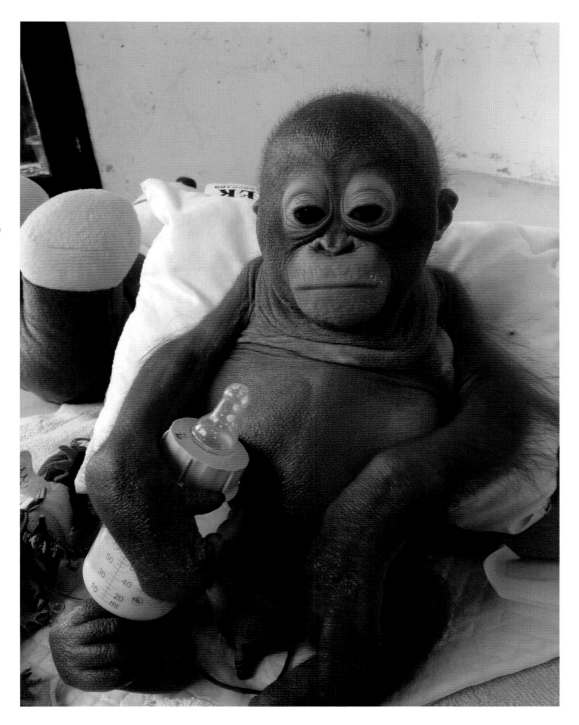

Budi is also being treated for a severe metabolic disease affecting his bones. His limbs are malformed due to malnutrition. (*please opposite page*)

Budi has a very long way to go on the road to recovery and it is still too early to know whether he has sustained any permanent damage. Meanwhile, he is receiving lots of love and care from the team at the rehabilitation centre.

Budi (left) has since struck up a friendship with another rescuee *Jemmi a*nd the two are now inseparable.

An increasingly important part of International Animal Rescue's work involves public awareness, specifically in West Kalimantan, but also across Indonesia in general. Empowering young, enthusiastic people to care about and protect 'their' orangutans and forest habitat is vitally important for the future. Thankfully, interest in conservation from young Indonesian people is greater than in any other south-east Asian nation, which gives us hope for the future. IAR in collaboration with a local Ketapang group are seen here calling on people to protect both orangutans and forests.

Preparing for a street demonstration on the annual 'Orangutan Day' in Ketapang. Three conservation organisations working together for the common goal of saving orangutans. International Animal Rescue, Yayasan Palung and Flora and Fauna International.

A locally arranged 'One Voice for Conservation' walk was very well supported by the younger generation and gives hope for the future.

One of the ways to create local interest in and concern for orangutans has been a drawing competition organised by International Animal Rescue and local group Yayasan Palung. This proved very popular with some of the participants seen here.

To help create greater public awareness and interest the best illustrations were selected and made into a calendar for free distribution in the area.

The owner had bought *Sigit* a few months before delivering him to the rehabilitation centre after becoming concerned about the baby's health. When handed over to IAR *Sigit* was wearing baby clothes and estimated to have been one and a half years old. He was the first orangutan to be rescued and placed in the one hectare fenced area used for baby school of IAR in Ketapang. As cute as this baby looks, in the wild he would sometimes sit like this with his mother high up in the forest canopy.

Orangutans are the only non-human apes remaining in all of Asia.

Sharing 96.4% of our DNA, like humans they also feel pain and are able to express fear, aggression, surprise and joy.

Pungky had been bought by a taxi driver and kept in a small cage. It had been so long since he had been out of his cage the owner had difficulty getting the lock open. *Pungky* has since settled in well at the rehabilitation centre, is a keen tree climber, but has also been known when nervous to chase staff and bite their ankles! *(please also see opposite page)*

Pungky putting on his sweet and innocent face which belies his sometimes mischievous behaviour.

While the rescuing and caring for orangutans continues, the IAR team also needs to look for forests with existing populations of orangutans. A boat is almost always necessary to reach such forests.

Life in the jungle is not as exciting as it may sound. The team's rudimentary home in the forest, shared by both male and female team members. Saving orangutans requires a lot of personal sacrifices as well as dedication.

Aside from coping with the basic eating and sleeping facilities, there are the long hours of trekking in silence through humid jungle full of insects waiting to feast on human flesh. While trying not to get lost, the team needs to stop occasionally to listen for signs of orangutans in the treetops.

This two to three year old named *Helen* was found on a palm oil plantation hogtied to a pole. She had clearly been brutally beaten by plantation workers who also killed her mother. *(please see overleaf.)*

Covered in cuts and bruises, *Helen* had been tied by her wrists and ankles to a pole and was just barely alive. She was also severely dehydrated and emaciated after being starved for days or even weeks. Despite everything she had endured *Helen* survived and after years of rehabilitation is now a healthy and independent orangutan living freely once again in a safe forest. *(please see the next two pages)*

After a remarkable recovery from her injuries followed by years of preparation, *Helen* is once again back in the wild where she belongs. *(please see next page)*

Before her release into a protected forest *Helen* was fitted with a transmitter to enable IAR staff to follow and record her activities to ensure she has the necessary skills to survive in the wild. She has made good progress, finding plenty of fruit to eat and showing no signs of wanting the company of her human rescuers.

For the good of their mental and physical health orphaned orangutans in the grounds of the rehabilitation centre are encouraged to search and climb to find food concealed, in this instance, inside a perforated ball.

Although intended as food containers, barrels have been adapted for use as resting places by some enterprising orangutans.

Ayu, one of the vets at the rehabilitation centre, is showing *Marie* it's safe to eat termites extracted from a freshly discovered nest.

Every day the orangutans also receive disposable enrichment items that are made for their immediate enjoyment. These are things like leaf parcels, happy sacks, boomer balls and hanging logs, which have small amounts of food hidden or wrapped inside them and are then hung in the trees. The orangutans have to work at getting to their food treat of seeds and nuts.

Enrichment (*please also see previous page*) is essential for all orangutans, regardless of age. Sadly, few zoos have yet to recognise how important and easy it is to provide enrichment, which is why visitors to zoos often see bored, even lonely looking orangutans staring back at them. It is hoped these photographs and their captions will enlighten and motivate zoo management and staff to make the lives of their captive orangutans so much more enriched.

Both orangutans know there's tasty food inside the rubber toy, but they have to work out how to extract it. It's a very important part of their rehabilitation programme.

The simplest and cheapest of things can keep a baby's mind occupied for a long time.

Searching for some tasty termites is a skill
Desi has learnt during her time at the centre.
When she is returned to the forest to start
a new life, termites will form an important
food resource.

A bowl of wood shavings provides the always inquisitive fun-loving orangutans with something to explore and play with. The more serious side of this is the very important need to keep these orphaned orangutans fully occupied all day long. There's even, by orangutan standards, an orderly queue for the large tub full of wood flakes to play in. l to r: *Melki, Ongky* & *Sigit*

Obi was a particularly tragic case. Estimated to have been three years old when confiscated, he had been kept on a one metre long chain in a toilet. Very pale in colour from being kept indoors for so long and fed on a diet of cake, sweets and soft drinks, *Obi* had become obese and aggressive. During his time in captivity he was not allowed outside and had only a small piece of rope above him to play with. He is now recovering well at the rehabilitation centre. *(Please see opposite page.)*

Obi's obesity is apparent but with a new lease of life involving nutritious food and lots of exercise he is steadily getting into better shape.

Considering the trauma he experienced in his first three years it's not surprising *Obi* not only distrusts people, he has even bitten three members of the rehabilitation team. These characteristics actually make him a good candidate for release.

According to local villagers, this orangutan had been roaming around the area for some time, going into small sugar cane plantations and eating the fruits from trees near their houses. A large male named *Alan*, around 15 years old, he was probably confused by the fact that the surrounding forest was vanishing, leaving the orangutans and many other species without a home or food. Once sedated by an anaesthetic dart he slowly began to climb down from the tree until just a metre off the ground when he finally fell slowly to the earth. *(please see opposite page.)*

Once the medical team pronounced *Alan* to be in good health it was decided the best thing would be to release him into a forest three hours away by boat. Manoeuvring a heavy crate containing a 70 to 80kg orangutan onto a small boat requires skill as well as strength. At the release site the crate was moved to the front of the boat to enable the orangutan to climb directly into the forest. Job done, it was a long way home by boat in the dark for the rescue team.

Having being kept as a pet for about a year, treated like a child, dressed and bathed, *Joyce* had become very humanised before she was confiscated and handed over to IAR to rehabilitate. *(please see opposite page).*

The rehabilitation of *Joyce* is well under way in forest school, preparing her for the day she will be released back into the forest.

When rescued this tiny baby was less than six months old and weighing only 2kg. The owner claimed he had found *Jemmi* alone in the forest. This is highly unlikely because such a young infant would never stray from its mother.

Marie literally arrived on the rehabilitation centre's doorstep one evening after being surrendered to IAR by her temporary owner. She was thin and very small for her age of around seven to nine months. The baby was found by a fisherman who was walking in the forest and heard crying. He said she was alone (which would be highly unusual) and when her mother did not come for her he took her back to his home. The man kept her for a couple of weeks, but when he could no longer afford to feed her he decided to hand her over to IAR. She had been bathed often, given rice and bananas to eat and milk to drink - sometimes the strawberry flavoured variety.

Marie (please also see previous page and opposite)

Although thin and very small for her age, probably due to malnourishment, *Marie* is showing some promising wild behaviour, as she climbs well on her hammock, likes to play with leaves, and loves to eat fruit.

Karmele Llano Sanchez

An accomplished vet with many years'
previous experience treating and caring for
primates, Karmele is programme director
of International Animal Rescue projects in
Indonesia. The success of the orangutan
rehabilitation centre is a testament
to her dedication, determination and
organisational skills.

To help prevent orangutans being killed or captured IAR has an ongoing programme to reduce and eventually eliminate conflict caused when orangutans come into contact with villagers and plantation workers. Meeting local people to discuss any issues they may have regarding orangutans is something Programme Manager Dr Gail Campbell-Smith does on a regular basis.

Paloma Corbí, Primatologist, monitors orangutans which have been released into a safe forest to ensure they are adapting well and able to cope on their own. The work begins when the orangutans wake at around 5:00am and ends when they make a night-nest about 5:00pm. The monitoring continues from 6 months to 2 years.

Lisa Burtenshaw is Orangutan Projects volunteer facilitator. Such is her passion for helping orangutans Lisa sold her business in the UK and now spends six months of the year training as well as helping volunteers.

Many volunteer hands do indeed make light work of preparing food for orangutans.

People travel from all over the world to help the orangutans cared for at the International Animal Rescue centre in Ketapang, West Borneo. It's a great opportunity to make a difference, make new friends, learn new skills and experience another culture. For details please see overleaf and contact both: **www.projectorangutan.com/tour/ketapang-project** and **www.thegreatprojects.com/projects/iar-orangutan-project**

Volunteers are key team members and they make a big difference by carrying out, among other things, essential maintenance work at the rehabilitation centre. Both the orangutans and the charity benefit greatly from the work done by volunteers. These enterprising people sometimes find themselves in all manner of places and positions they could never have imagined back home.

Volunteers might one day be making a sturdy hammock for an orangutan to sleep in and the next day building a bridge over a canal to a future forest home for the orphans. Whatever the work, volunteers have fun while obtaining an enormous amount of satisfaction from making a difference to the lives of orangutans.

A big thank you to sponsors and supporters from International Animal Rescue Borneo-based staff and volunteers March 2015

Glossary

We hope the following explanations will help you obtain the most interest and pleasure from reading Orangutan Rescue.

Transit centre: This refers to a small centre in Ketapang which International Animal Rescue (IAR) took over from a local environmental organisation in November 2009. It soon became clear the number of rescued orangutans would exceed the capacity of the transit centre; plans were put in place to build a new centre.

Rehabilitation centre: Thanks to the generosity of supporters IAR was able to buy 24 hectares of land and build a permanent rescue and rehabilitation centre not far from the transit centre. A further 42 hectares of land have since been bought. During 2013 all the orangutans were transferred to the new facility and the transit centre was closed. The new centre can accommodate up to 100 orangutans at a time and facilities include a large quarantine building for new arrivals, fully-equipped veterinary clinic, a public education centre, indoor accommodation for adult and baby orangutans and spacious outdoor forested enclosures where they can develop the skills and natural behaviour they will need to fend for themselves in the wild.

Quarantine: All newly confiscated orangutans are quarantined. This may last from six to eight weeks, sometimes a little less for babies. This is to enable vets to check the orangutans' health thoroughly and ensure no parasites or diseases such as TB or hepatitis are brought into the centre.

Forestry police: Only the police have the legal powers to confiscate orangutans. The police attend every confiscation.

Babysitters: These are local people trained and employed by IAR to care for baby orangutans at the centre until they are capable of moving on to forest school.

Baby school: A one hectare area of enclosed forest the baby orangutans are taken to play in and explore every day under close supervision of their babysitters. The behaviour of individual babies is observed and recorded. Their level of confidence, ability and independence will influence when they are to be moved to join older orangutans in forest school.

Forest school: Forty hectares of enclosed forest where the more able but still largely human dependent orangutans can socialise, develop their climbing skills and begin searching for their own wild food. Most of these orangutans return to the centre in the evening, but occasionally a more independent one will stay in the forest and build a nest for the night.

Enrichment: A variety of things from climbing frames, hammocks to rest in, food and toys provided to keep the highly intelligent and inquisitive orangutans from becoming bored. Also used to teach young orangutans how to search for food.

Names of orangutans: Every orangutan that comes into the centre is given a name. This enables staff to monitor their individual development and health. Extensive records are maintained to ensure nothing is missed that might in any way jeopardise their rehabilitation.

International Animal Rescue (IAR)

UK Charity Registration Number: 1118277
United States Registered 501(c)(3) non-profit organization, Tax Id: 54-2044674

At International Animal Rescue we do exactly what our name says – we save animals from suffering around the world. Our work includes cutting free and caring for dancing bears in India, rescuing orangutans and other primates in distress in Indonesia and sterilising and vaccinating stray dogs and cats in developing countries. Wherever possible we return rescued animals to their natural environment but we also provide a permanent home for animals that can no longer fend for themselves.

As human populations expand, wildlife is coming under increasing threat. By rescuing individual animals belonging to endangered species like the orangutan and reintroducing them into protected areas in the wild, our work plays a role in the conservation of the species as a whole.

We work to educate the public in the compassionate and humane treatment of all animals. Sound scientific evidence forms the basis for our decision-making and determines the course of our rescue operations. In all that we do we aim to find practical solutions that benefit both animals and people. We also work with other like-minded organisations and government departments to strengthen legislation to protect animals from cruelty and neglect.

Head Office: International Animal Rescue has its head office in the UK. Our small team of administrators, fundraisers and supporter care staff work closely with our teams in the field to ensure the projects run smoothly.

International Animal Rescue, US: International Animal Rescue, US was incorporated on 19 April 2001 and subsequently registered in every state in the USA. This enabled us to start raising awareness of our projects and generate funds to support them through a programme of direct mail appeals to animal-loving members of the public. By means of this programme we are building up a network of people eager to support our projects and help us spread the word about our vital work.

Since 2006 International Animal Rescue has run a small administrative office in Massachusetts. During the latter half of 2014, with the transfer of a member of our UK fundraising team to the US, we increased our presence there and started to engage new audiences.

Adoptions: One very popular way to support our work is by taking out a virtual adoption of one of the animals in our care. Our online gallery of orangutans available for adoption includes JoJo, Monti, Rickina, Joyce, Gunung and most recently Budi. As well as a certificate, factsheet and photo of your adopted animal, plus an optional soft toy, adopters are given access to exclusive updates, images and videos.

An adoption is the perfect way to stay in touch with our projects and help to provide regular, reliable income to support them. To find out more please visit: **www.internationalanimalrescue.org/adopt-an-animal** or telephone (UK) **01825 767688** (USA) **508 826 1083**